W9-CPB-946

Pebble® Plus

Backyard Birds

House Sparrows

by Lisa J. Amstutz

Consulting Editor:
Gail Saunders-Smith, PhD

Consultant: André Dhondt,
Morgens Professor of Ornithology,
Cornell Laboratory of Ornithology

CAPSTONE PRESS
a capstone imprint

Pebble Plus is published by Capstone Press,
1710 Roe Crest Drive, North Mankato, Minnesota 56003
www.capstonepub.com

Library of Congress Cataloging-in-Publication Data
Amstutz, Lisa J., author.
 House sparrows / by Lisa J. Amstutz.
   pages cm. -- (Pebble plus. Backyard birds)
 Summary: "Simple text and full-color photographs introduce house sparrows"—Provided
by publisher.
 Audience: Ages 5-7
 Audience: K to grade 3
Includes bibliographical references and index.
 ISBN 978-1-4914-6109-9 (library binding)
 ISBN 978-1-4914-6113-6 (paperback)
 ISBN 978-1-4914-6117-4 (eBook PDF)
1. House sparrow--Juvenile literature. I. Title.
 QL696.P264A47 2016
 598.8'87—dc23   2015001328

Editorial Credits
Elizabeth R. Johnson, editor; Bobbie Nuytten, designer;
Svetlana Zhurkin, media researcher; Tori Abraham, production specialist

Photo Credits
Dreamstime: Catherine Downie, 7, William Attard Mccarthy, 15; iStockphoto: Westhoff, 17;
Shutterstock: Anatoliy Lukich, 21, Andrew Williams, cover (inset), 1 (inset), cpaulfell, 11,
dmitriyGo, 13, Flegere, cover (back), 1 (back), 2—3, 24, GDM, 4 and throughout, Stephen
Meese, 9, Vasily Vishnevskiy, 5; SuperStock: FLPA, 19

Note to Parents and Teachers

The Backyard Birds set supports national curriculum standards for science related to
life science and ecosystems. This book describes and illustrates house sparrows. The
images support early readers in understanding the text. The repetition of words and
phrases helps early readers learn new words. This book also introduces early readers
to subject-specific vocabulary words, which are defined in the Glossary section. Early
readers may need assistance to read some words and to use the Table of Contents,
Glossary, Read More, Internet Sites, Critical Thinking Using the Common Core, and
Index sections of the book.

Printed in the United States of America in North Mankato, Minnesota.
032015   008823CGF15

Table of Contents

All About House Sparrows

Cheep, cheep, cheep!

House sparrows make lots of noise.

They hop and peck at seeds.

House sparrows are 6 to 7 inches

(15 to 18 centimeters) long.

Females are brown with stripes.

Males are dark brown and gray,

with a black bib.

male

female

The birds eat grain and seeds.

They eat crumbs that people drop.

They eat some insects too.

Where House Sparrows Live

House sparrows live in

many parts of the world.

People brought them to

North America to eat pests.

Now they are very common.

House sparrows live in cities and fields. They like to live near people and farm animals. They eat and sleep together in flocks.

House sparrows make nests in holes. They stuff the holes with dried plants, feathers, and string. They nest in trees, roofs, and even traffic lights.

The Life of a House Sparrow

The female lays four to six speckled eggs. She sits on them to keep them warm. The chicks hatch in two weeks.

At first the chicks are helpless.

Their parents bring them food.

The chicks grow fast.

They leave the nest

in about two weeks.

Look for house sparrows

in your backyard!

House Sparrow Range

Year-round

*range shown in North America

Glossary

chick—a young bird

flock—a group of animals that live, travel, and eat together

grain—the seed of a cereal plant, like oats or wheat

hatch—to break out of an egg

insect—a small animal with a hard outer shell, six legs, three body sections, and two antennae; house sparrows eat beetles, caterpillars, and aphids

nest—a place to lay eggs and bring up young

pest—an animal that hurts or bothers people; insects and mice can be pests

speckled—marked with small spots or patches of color

Read More

Alderfer, Jonathan. *National Geographic Kids Bird Guide of North America*. Washington, D.C.: National Geographic, 2013.

Kurki, Kim. *National Wildlife Federation's World of Birds: A Beginner's Guide*. New York: Black Dog & Leventhal Publishers, 2014.

Russo, Monica. *Birdology: 30 Activities and Observations for Exploring the World of Birds*. Chicago: Chicago Review Press, 2015.

Internet Sites

FactHound offers a safe, fun way to find Internet sites related to this book. All of the sites on FactHound have been researched by our staff.

Here's all you do:

Visit *www.facthound.com*

Type in this code: 9781491461099

Super-cool stuff! Check out projects, games and lots more at **www.capstonekids.com**

Critical Thinking
Using the Common Core

1. Where do house sparrows build their nests? (Key Ideas and Details)

2. Do house sparrows live alone or with other birds? (Key Ideas and Details)

3. Look at the photo on page 9. What is the house sparrow eating? (Integration of Knowledge and Ideas)

Index

Word Count: 182
Grade: 1
Early-Intervention Level: 14